Planning the Life You |
Living the Life You Deserve

Creating & Achieving Goals That Matter Most

By Marcia Elder

Published By: CPI Consulting ~ www.CPICorporate.com

Copyright © November 2015 by Marcia Elder. All rights reserved. No part of this publication may be reproduced, distributed, or transmitted in any form or by any means, including photocopying, recording, or other electronic, mechanical or other methods, without the prior written permission of the publisher, except in the case of brief quotations embodied in published critical reviews and certain other noncommercial uses permitted by copyright law. For permission requests, write to the publisher.

No specific results are being suggested or guaranteed by the author. Readers are responsible for defining and creating their own life results and the methods of achieving those results. The book can serve as a valuable resource for use by readers toward that end.

Published By: CPI Consulting ~ www.CPICorporate.com

Note to Readers

This book embodies a "process" of planning and personal development. A process for creating positive change in your life, for now and the rest of your life. Workbook-style forms are included as part of the process. The forms are intended to be filled out for the purpose of defining your dreams, planning your future and achieving your goals. The book has been published using 8 X 10 pages as the most practical size for this use and includes additional space for your personal notes.

Resolution setting as an annual tradition for many inspired the book. But its content goes well beyond resolutions ... to the even more important needs of finding out our purpose, what we really want from our lives and how to have, do and be what we most desire.

It is a book meant to be referred to throughout the year ... and used for years to come in planning for your life and carrying out the plans you create. What you create through the process of this book can become your compass to guide the way to your best self and your best life.

The content of your forms and notes are like your own personal diary or journal. Treat them as such. Some people choose to share them with loved ones and others as a way of being closer and seeking support. For others the information is strictly private. If so for you then keep it in a private place or make known that it is off-limits to others. Perhaps you will decide to share it at a later time, or not at all. Whatever your choice, the process made possible through this book is a personal one for and about you and your future. Enjoy it, savor it and make the very most of it.

Access to a **Bonus Gift** plus other timely resources for readers are provided in Chapter 17 of the book. Also find out here how to get **electronic versions** of the workbook forms: www.CPICorporate.com/workbook-forms/.

Tribute to Stephen Covey

Stephen Covey was a master at planning for the very best in life. His books and other works leave a timeless legacy for others to learn from, be inspired by and, most importantly, act upon. This book is dedicated to him in thanks for his many and vast contributions.

Stephen Richards Covey (October 24, 1932 – July 16, 2012) was a celebrated educator, author, businessman and leader. His most popular book was "The Seven Habits of Highly Effective People". Some of his other books include "Living the 7 Habits", "First Things First", "Principle-Centered Leadership", "The 7 Habits of Highly Effective Families" and "The 8th Habit, From Effectiveness to Greatness". He was a professor at Utah State University at the time of his death. He died at the age of 79 due to complications from a bicycling accident. *Source: Wikipedia*

Table of Contents

NOTE TO READERS	III
TRIBUTE TO STEPHEN COVEY	IV
PART I: LAYING THE GROUNDWORK/DESIGNING YOUR LIFE	**1**
CHAPTER 1 ~ ABOUT THE BOOK	3
CHAPTER 2 ~ RESOLUTIONS & WHY THEY MATTER	5
CHAPTER 3 ~ THE WHAT, WHY & HOW	7
CHAPTER 4 ~ MAKING LASTING CHANGES	9
CHAPTER 5 ~ BUFFET OF OPTIONS	13
CHAPTER 6 ~ REAL WORLD CASE STUDY	17
CHAPTER 7 ~ STRATEGIES FOR GOALS & RESOLUTIONS	21
CHAPTER 8 ~ YOUR NEXT STEPS!	25
PART II. TOOL KIT FOR SUCCESS: PLANNING YOUR FUTURE, ACHIEVING YOUR GOALS	**27**
CHAPTER 9 ~ PURPOSE & USES OF "TOOL KIT"	29
CHAPTER 10 ~ MY PURPOSE IN LIFE	33
CHAPTER 11 ~ MY GOALS & PRIORITIES	37
CHAPTER 12 ~ CREATING MY RESOLUTIONS	85
CHAPTER 13 ~ STRATEGIES FOR ACHIEVING MY GOALS & RESOLUTIONS	97
CHAPTER 14 ~ ACTION STEPS: THE STEPS TO CARRY OUT MY CHARGE	103
CHAPTER 15 ~ IMPLEMENTATION: ACHIEVING ULTIMATE SUCCESS	107
CHAPTER 16 ~ MONITORING MY PROGRESS	113
CHAPTER 17 ~ BONUS RESOURCES	127
APPENDIX	**131**
BACKGROUND	131
RESOLUTIONS	132
SAMPLE PLANS	135
ABOUT THE AUTHOR	141
ABOUT THE PUBLISHER	142
REVIEWS & OTHER BOOKS	143

We each have the power to determine the quality of our lives. Claim your power and use this book to create the life you truly want. In the words of Anthony Robbins: "*Unleash the Power Within*".

To continue the process even further, check out www.CPICorporate.com/creating-the-life/

Insights from Inspirational Leaders

Words of wisdom from great leaders appear throughout this book. Think about their meaning and how they can bring value as you embark on the process laid out in this book.

"Begin with the end in mind."

Stephen Covey

"By recording your dreams and goals on paper, you set in motion the process of becoming the person you most want to be."

Mark Victor Hansen

"What you get by achieving your goals is not as important as what you become by achieving your goals."

Zig Ziglar

"Goals in writing are dreams with deadlines."

Brian Tracy

"People with goals succeed because they know where they're going."

Earl Nightingale

"If you can dream it, you can do it."

Walt Disney

Part I:
Laying the Groundwork
Designing Your Life

Keys to Success:

The first step to success is to define what "success" means to you ... not just in the moment but for how you use the limited time you have on this earth ... how you live your life, who you have in your life, what you bring to the world, who you are as a person. The more clarity you have the more fruitful the journey on your path to success.

Setting goals and priorities that really matter & taking effective action to achieve them ... these are the path to success.

Chapter 1 ~ About the Book

Imagine that you can have what you most want in your life ... just by taking steps within your power on your own behalf.

Whether your dreams and goals are grandiose or simple, three key ingredients to achieving them are these: **deciding that they (and you) are worth it ... taking *action* to make them real ... and taking *effective* action.**

This book is about getting the best results for you and your life. It provides insights, concrete examples and specific tools toward that important end.

"New Year's Resolutions" started out as the planned theme for the book ... and now the final version goes way further. **Part I lays out the "big picture" for having what you want in life.** It sets the foundation for planning the life you desire and creating the life you deserve. **Part II is a "workbook" to help you chart your course, embark upon it and stick to it.** The forms in the workbook are "timeless" – they can be used over and again.

Years ago I committed to an annual process of evaluating the past and planning for the future that has gotten powerful results in my life. I've used variations of it at the end of each year for over two decades and I've put it to work all year-round. The process is one that can be undertaken at any time – all that's required is a commitment. I'm happy to share the basic process with you in this book (which you can add to or adapt to best meet your personal needs) and I hope that it brings you great value too.

Setting meaningful goals that will be achieved and resolutions <u>that will be kept</u> involves honest evaluation and strategic planning. It's something that anyone can do, and having a system for doing so makes all the difference.

If you're thinking "I'm not the kind of person" who sets goals, makes resolutions or does "strategic planning", think again and give it a try. You will likely be quite surprised by what you can create and accomplish in doing so. If you already do so, here's the chance to improve on your approach for even better results in your life.

Don't you owe it to yourself (and perhaps others who you care about and who care about you) to make your goals reality and live your life to the fullest? Take action now!

Note: "Creating the Life You Desire" was written in 2013 and published with limited updates in 2015 with worldwide access through Amazon.com.

Keys to Success:

With imagination we can design our best future …
… with resolve we can create it.

Chapter 2 ~ Resolutions & Why They Matter

As mentioned, the book began with a focus on resolutions ... and it evolved into a book of grander scope, including life goals, personal strategic planning and specific strategies and actions for transforming desires into reality. Resolutions are one piece of life planning and transformation.

Resolutions are statements of resolve ... pinpointing actions that a person resolves or commits to take. Their purpose is as a tool for achieving new end results in the person's life, to make things better in one way or another.

New Year's Resolutions are a tradition ... one that makes good sense. The "new" year signals new beginnings and such resolutions are geared to actions that will be taken and results achieved during the course of the year.

Of course, resolutions are not limited to being kicked off on January 1. They can have lasting value no matter when they're set and acted upon.

Resolutions are not the end goal. They are actions we commit to in order to achieve our larger goals. Resolving to stop smoking, for example, more than likely ties to a broader goal related to health, longevity or appearance.

Resolutions represent a key step on the path to positive change ... the path that, if committed to, can take us to where we most want to be in our lives.

Being clear about our goals is the first step to creating meaningful and powerful resolutions and results.

Every year (and every day) we have the opportunity to make our lives better through setting and keeping resolutions.

Keys to Success:

A compelling reason ... a strong enough why ... makes all the difference in the world to *having* the lives we desire.

Chapter 3 ~ The What, Why & How

Stephen Covey was the master at helping people achieve their goals through gaining a clear understanding of the "What, Why and How" of whatever it was they were seeking to do. He always put the What and Why first – knowing what you want and why it matters to you, before being concerned about the How.

As Covey would point out, people tend to want to jump head first into the How (the activities of pursuing something) before being certain of what they really want. Spelling out the Why sometimes reveals that what we thought we wanted isn't really all that important to us, or at least not the most important compared to other things.

He noted that if you have a strong enough Why, the How (to make it happen) will naturally follow. The Why provides the motivation, the juice, the force for getting things done, for pursuing what we want and achieving our goals.

Covey's approach works wonders. And, in keeping with it, goals and the desired outcomes we're each seeking are part of the first order of business for the process laid out in this book.

What do we want?

What do _you_ want?

Once we know that – and we test and solidify it by spelling out the Why – defining the How comes next ... including the specific strategies and steps involved, the course we will take to make the goals or dreams real.

Keys to Success:

Are you "interested" in achieving your dreams ... or are you *absolutely committed*? Ask yourself, how are the two so very different (how specifically) for what you want in your life?

Chapter 4 ~ The Process of Making Lasting Changes

There's an age-old saying about when the student is ready the teacher shows up. The "teacher" (someone from whom we can learn important lessons) may be around all the time. But if the person with the opportunity to learn doesn't realize it, or doesn't want to learn ... that person is not likely to learn.

Life is a process of learning and growth. Growth involves change. Yet, most people resist change ... whether by not seeing the need for it, or feeling it's too hard or uncomfortable, or feeling fear or doubt about their abilities, or objecting to someone else who's pushing them to change when they don't want to change or be pushed. These and other reasons can stand in the way of needed or worthwhile change.

Change often feels uncomfortable in one way or another. So as "creatures of comfort" and of habit we often "avoid it like the plague". Instead, we do what we're used to – even when that doesn't serve us (or others) well.

For many people who do make changes the changes don't last. Dieting, then losing weight but gaining it right back, is a good example.

"Change is a part of realizing goals & resolutions."

For changes to occur, and to last, takes the following ingredients:

1. Clearly define the desired change and why you want it
2. Commit to making the change
3. Develop an effective strategy for getting the results you seek
4. Identify the specific steps you will take
5. "Work your plan"

If a spouse or someone else wants you to make a change but you don't want to, you may make it, or make some effort toward it, but chances are the change won't stick. In some cases it may if the person makes pleasing the other person (who wants them to change) more important than their own wants or needs. But if it's something you object to or really don't want, resentment or other bad feelings may occur, creating a new issue to be dealt with apart from the change itself.

If the change is something you know you "should" do, but you really don't want to, there's also a challenge to making it work. One of the ways around that is to tap new strategies, such as asking yourself empowering questions. Questions like "how good or great am I going to feel when I achieve 'xyz'?" and "how good/great are my loved ones (or friends, co-workers, etc.) going to feel?". Or how bad will I or they feel if I don't? Applying imagination in the process (to the point of really feeling it) can easily get you to feel enough of a "good" or "bad" emotion to make the change.

Ask yourself the questions that are relevant to you and answer them with sincerity and in specificity. Then visualize the result in place. Imagine yourself taking steps and, then, having achieved your goals and resolutions. Picture in detail the process as well as the achievement.

Committing to make your goals and resolutions take place is a vital ingredient. If you're only "interested" in doing so, rather than truly committed, the results will likely reflect that ... by being incomplete, ineffective, temporary, etc. By contrast, the decision to change is backed by a power that can take you right where you want to be, the power of action.

Also important: you can *want* to change all day long and you can accompany that desire by a sincere and concerted effort. But if you have the wrong strategy (and action steps), success will likely pass you by.

Say, for example, your goal was to lose 30 pounds and your strategy was to walk every day. That sounds good ... until you map out your walking route to include passing by the bakery -- where you "just can't resist" the smell of freshly baked pastries and you justify having one (or more) each day, since you'll be "walking it off"! Justifying having a pastry or two (or their equivalent) after you walk, perhaps as a reward for your having walked, likewise can defeat one's purpose.

Integrating your strategies in a way that advances your multiple goals is important as well. For instance, if one of your goals is to cut back on spending and the other is to lose weight, with a strategy of walking ... making your laps in the shopping mall (as some people do) may not be the best plan if you have difficulty disciplining yourself as you pass by the many storefronts. If that's you, choose a place that makes you feel good while supporting rather than conflicting with your goals.

"Working your plan" means just that ... taking charge, carrying it out with discipline and vigor ... being accountable to yourself for making steady progress and reaching your target. If you regularly "let yourself off the hook" you're not really committed and not holding yourself sufficiently accountable to get where you want to go.

If you really want to make a change, define and "see" your goals and resolutions with clarity ... resolve to make them yours ... map out an effective plan and charge forth on the path to victory!

Keys to Success:

Imagination enables creation. Imagine a goal as though you have achieved it. See it in your mind's eye in specific detail ... imagine the feelings you will experience ... and how your life will be so much better once it is achieved.

Inspirational Insights

"Goals allow you to control the direction of change in your favor."
Brian Tracy

"If you don't know where you are going, you'll probably end up somewhere else."
Lewis Carroll

"Goals that are not written down are just wishes."
Anonymous

"The establishment of a clear, central purpose or goal in life is the starting point of all success."
Brian Tracy

"I find it fascinating that most people plan their vacations with better care than they do their lives. Perhaps that is because escape is easier than change."
Jim Rohn

Chapter 5 ~ A Buffet of Options

For most if not all who are reading this book, there are many options for goals and resolutions to enhance our lives. A buffet or even cornucopia of them. Likewise, there is an array of steps we each can take within and outside of ourselves to be, do and create more for our present and future.

When it comes to both goals and resolutions, most people want to:

- Stop something
- Start something
- Become something or
- Get something

A range of examples includes:

Stop something

- Smoking
- Overeating
- Drinking
- Doing drugs
- Over-spending
- Cursing
- Gambling
- Bad relationship
- Losing one's temper

Start something

- Learn a new skill (how to play the guitar, ballroom dancing, how to use more features on your I-phone, connecting on social media, etc.)
- Create a new business or get a new job

- Find a new relationship
- Take a current relationship in a new direction
- Undertake an enjoyable hobby
- Join a club or team (book club, tennis team, social group, etc.)

Become something

- Feel more confidence (rather than fearfulness)
- Experience peace (overcoming worry, distraction, disempowering emotions)
- Simplify your life (become free by getting rid of clutter, getting organized, lessening your attachment to "things")
- Be loving – express love to others
- Accept love from others
- Be truthful and direct with others
- Achieve more balance

Get something

- Buy a new home, car, etc.
- Earn a promotion or raise at work
- Win a prize in a contest or competition
- Earn a degree or certification
- Be acknowledged by family, friends
- Receive an award

These may or may not be on your list. They are here to get you thinking about what is or will be.

In creating your list (as will come in Part II), be sure to connect whatever your resolutions are back to the goals they relate to. The goals come first. The resolutions, strategies and action steps are ways of achieving the goals.

There are many alternatives for goals and resolutions. And each of us has only so much time, energy, resources and other capabilities to go after them. So choose with that in mind.

Don't be shy in having multiple priorities on your "list". But also don't load yourself up to the point that you don't get anything done. And know, of course, that some will be easier to tackle than others. Some may indeed be painfully difficult ... though well worth the effort. You must be the judge of what they're each worth considering the specific benefits of your actions.

It all comes down to what's most important to you and what are you able to manage at any particular point in time. Also know this: that, if we put our minds and emotions to it, we can often do much more than we give ourselves credit for.

Whatever is on your list, **structure your goals and resolutions for success**. Part II of this book is a great resource for crafting both to meet your needs and serve you best. A real life case study also follows in the next Chapter.

Keys to Success:

Knowing what you want is a fundamental step to getting it ... most often we have to realize it in order to *"real-ize"* it (make it real). What do you most want?

"Do not go where the path may lead;

Go instead where there is no path and leave a trail."

Ralph Waldo Emerson

Chapter 6 ~ Real World Case Study

Often it's helpful to know of specific examples and actual stories where people have made changes in their lives. So here's one from my own life to illustrate key ingredients to change: **The Goal, The Why** (it's important), **The Resolution, The Action Steps and Strategy** (for achieving it) plus **The Results**. It's a simple example with parts that no doubt many can relate to.

~

In the process of family caregiving I gained 35 pounds. I was sedentary at the time, compared to my normal very active life. My diet was poor and I was eating whatever was fast and easy. I rarely looked in the mirror and didn't even notice what was happening to my body (as was the least of my concerns). But over the course of a year or so, the pounds had poured on.

I've always been pretty much a slender person and (after I emerged from the caregiving process) that amount of added weight was quite noticeable, to me and others. It made me feel bad, physically (less fit, heavy, less endurance) and in appearance. I also could no longer fit into most of my clothes (other than PJs, sweat pants and over-sized t-shirts). I wanted and needed a change. So what was my goal and what did I resolve?

My Goal

To recapture my physical vitality, improve my health and enhance my appearance.

The Why

I want to feel the full energy that I've always been accustomed to experiencing ... an energy level that enables me to lead a very active life, to be exuberant, to keep up with the many demands of my business, to make and keep commitments that allow me to make a difference in the world. I want to know that I'm taking good care of my physical health, as my health enables me in so many ways to achieve my purpose in life. I want to feel happy with the way I look and I want to look (and be) happy, for myself and because happy energy makes others feel good.

My Resolution

I resolve to lose 25 pounds over the next two years and at least 10 pounds this year.

My Action Steps

- Sign up for and attend a weekly high energy exercise class
- Lift weights at home twice per week
- Dance once per week (2 hours plus)
- Stop eating high-fat processed foods
- Regularly prepare meals and snacks made from fresh vegetables and fruits (and learn how to do more of that)
- Learn more about the fat content of foods and develop a diet to help me achieve my goals (using a book that I purchased on the subject)

My Strategy

I had never been on a diet before and the idea of doing so was less than appealing. I also was "too busy" to add an exercise regime to my schedule, much less to have to "learn how to cook" rather than popping frozen meals in the microwave.

But I knew that, **to get a new result I had to take new actions**. So I focused full force on my "empowering Why" ... and that's what it took to move me forward.

I also set a goal that was realistic. While I could have said I would lose the full 35 pounds in a year or even 6 months, I knew that wouldn't have happened. Commitments following the long period of caregiving were massive, on multiple fronts, and I knew I could only commit to so much in the way of new resolution steps that would take time and energy to implement. But I also was determined to carve out a certain amount of time each week to move forward on this goal.

I welcomed feedback from others (who typically said I was "too thin" before and that having some more weight was healthier and looked better) and in part based upon it I became comfortable with a loss of 25 pounds as the final target.

With that set, I then pushed myself to go after the target ... and within the bounds of what was appropriate for me, all things considered (including the fact that I always have multiple resolutions in the works).

The Results

I lost 10 pounds in the first year. While I had wanted to lose more, it still felt great. I signed up for a Zumba class and went twice (instead of once) per week. I did ballroom dancing once a week (mostly the fast variety, which I love). I cut the fatty frozen meals from my diet plus other foods that weren't serving me well – and I started learning how to prepare some tasty and healthy foods and drinks using fresh foods and other healthy choices. I attended a nutrition class that helped get me focused on effective options. I also used the above-mentioned food book (on calories and nutritional content) to get better informed. I did the weights on and off rather than weekly but I added in some power walking. I also scheduled several doctor's appointments that had been pushed to the back burner.

Bottom line: I achieved the goal and the resolution for year 1.

This particular resolution spanned 2 years and year 2 is now underway (with the resolution having been set mid-year – rather than the norm for me of January 1). The weight goal for this year is bigger and my schedule is even tighter. The Zumba class was cancelled and that was a big setback. My dance partner and I had our ups and downs and I'm dancing less than before. My work has me doing lots of writing and online work (sedentary). My metabolism changed significantly a couple of years back, making it all the harder to shed the weight.

The pressure is on! Can I do it? Absolutely! In fact just typing these words and "hearing" them come out of me is prompting me to stop writing and go for an invigorating walk. Back in a bit!

Keys to Success:

Having a *strategy* – with a method, approach, plan, tool, tactics and/ or system – for getting to where you want to be will greatly expedite the process … and make it do-able where it otherwise may well not be.

Chapter 7 ~ Strategies for Setting & Keeping Goals & Resolutions

As noted earlier, knowing what you want and why you want it are the foundation for your goals and resolutions as well as the strategies to carry them out. Some other steps for success follow:

- **Questions** - Ask yourself effective questions to help you understand what you really want. Many struggle with the discovery process. As I've seen time and again through my work in personal growth/professional development seminars and coaching, many who "think" they know what they want (at the start of the process) end up finding that what they really want is quite different. Good questions can help bring out what you most need to know. *Some examples follow later.*

- **Clarity** - The clearer we are in defining and describing our goals and resolutions (plus the strategies and actions), the greater the impact they will have. Being vague or "fuzzy" about them lacks the direction needed to manifest them.

- **Perspective** – Just because we want something now doesn't mean we will five years from now, or that we have in the past. Our needs change over time and so do the "things" we want to be, do and have. Don't be afraid to want something you never have before. Allow yourself to "dream big" for whatever it is you want.

- **Priorities** – Most of us want to "have, do and be" many different things. But as the saying goes, if we try to do "everything" we'll probably end up with disappointing results. The importance of each "thing" is relative to the other things on our list. Choose those you're ready to focus on now and keep the others in the queue for future action (if they remain important enough).

- **Write It** – The likelihood of your achieving your goals is greatly boosted by this simple step: write it down. Write down (or type up) your goals, resolutions, priorities, strategies and action steps. The written word will be something you can look at regularly as both a guide and reinforcement for your new directions. The more you look at it the greater the reinforcement. Checking it out once a day at a minimum will do wonders!

- **Team** – Sharing your goal and resolutions with others can help you stick to them. Some of the people in our lives can be called upon to provide reminders and cheer us on. Most of us also want to carry through on what we say we're going to do … and this puts us "on the line" to do so. Public testimonials can do so as well, like I've done in the above Case Study … the heat is on!

- **Progress** – Short of a very simple goal, or single easy-to-achieve resolution, we generally can't accomplish it all at once, and trying to do so can lead to frustration and giving up. Making progress is the key … recognizing that every step in the right direction counts. Evaluating how we're doing along the way also enables us to adjust and adapt as needed to get to the ultimate goal line … and to feel good about how far we've come.

- **Enjoy the Process** – Remember that the journey can be just as important as the destination. We learn from the process and as we learn we grow as individuals. Enjoy the ride. And be sure to acknowledge and reward yourself for a job well done!

More strategies and insights are available online at the link in the closing Chapter, including additional tools for your success.

FOR YOUR NOTES, IDEAS, PLANS, INSPIRATIONS ...

Planning the Life You Desire, Living the Life You Deserve

Creating & Achieving Goals That Matter Most

Inspirational Insights

"Without goals, and plans to reach them, you are like a ship that has set sail with no destination."
Fitzhugh Dodson

"This one step - choosing a goal and sticking to it - changes everything."
Scott Reed

"We aim above the mark to hit the mark."
Ralph Waldo Emerson

"Aim for the top. There is plenty of room there. There are so few at the top it is almost lonely there."
Samuel Insull

"From a certain point onward there is no longer any turning back. That is the point that must be reached."
Franz Kafka

Chapter 8 ~ Your Next Steps!

What are your goals? Why are they important to you? What do you resolve to do in order to make them happen? What will be your strategies and action steps?

These are the key questions for creating the life you desire and living the life you deserve.

Reflect on what you've read thus far ... where your life is now ... and possibilities for the future.

Life is a continuum of opportunity for more and better. What does that consist of for you ... within yourself and who you are as a person, in your relationships, in your work or avocation and in the other aspects of life that are important to you?

Believe in yourself and your ability to take new steps for the better ... even if your life is already good or great!

A one-of-a-kind tool for helping you do just that follows as Part II of this book.

Use this process to do something good and important for yourself ... including if that means setting it up with variations to what I've presented. Make the process your own.

We can't always control our external environment (what others say and do, the things happening around us and such). But **we CAN direct the focus of our minds and emotions**, and thereby our *experience* of life.

Part II. Tool Kit for Success: Planning Your Future, Achieving Your Goals

NOTE: Electronic versions of the workbook forms are available at www.CPICorporate.com/workbook-forms/. However, studies have shown that **the act of manually writing down one's ideas, plans and other notes increases retention of the information.** We encourage you to do just that ...

... to use this as a "workbook", to capture your thoughts on the pages throughout. Add drawings if you like, stickers, color highlighters, scribbles in the margins, whatever emerges from your personal process ... whatever reflects where you are, what you want, where you're going and how you'll get there ... plus the "why" for your plan and commitments.

Create something fabulous!

"Don't ask what the world needs. Ask what makes you come alive and go do that because what the world needs is people who have come alive." ~Howard Thurman

Chapter 9 ~ Purpose & Uses of This Kit

The Tool Kit is about making positive changes in your life.

It's designed to be your guide and support in doing so, through the steps you'll be taking in setting and achieving your goals and resolutions.

Just like resolutions, goals can be set at the start of a New Year ... or at any time. The important thing is to create them and make them happen. And "there's no time like the present" to get started.

The Tool Kit is totally user-friendly. And it's based on the assumption that the user, You, is ready to take action in support of your future.

Forms and exercises are provided toward that end along with a variety of examples and case studies to get you started ... and keep you moving. Some of the examples appear in the Appendix (Part III) and would be good to peruse before tackling the forms that begin in Chapter 11.

The Tool Kit can be used to whatever extent you choose ... from setting New Year's Resolutions to developing **your own personal Strategic Plan ... with your Purpose, Goals, Strategies and related action steps**, as an integrated approach to creating the results you desire for your life. I encourage you to take it the whole way!

The process can be done in a single day or you may prefer, or need, to break it into more than one sitting. You may need time to reflect on the questions and to consider possibilities. Either way, schedule one or more appointments with yourself to get the job done.

Your actions in using this Kit can reap great rewards for your future, in the year ahead and beyond. Indeed, **this system can be used year-in and**

year-out for as many goals, plans and resolutions as you may have throughout your life!

Create the time and private space where you can <u>focus on You</u> and great things to come for your life.

TIP: **Date each form page at the bottom** as you complete them. This will come in handy as you later evaluate your progress.

Also: the forms have been designed to benefit any and all who use them… as part of a proven-effective step-by-step process. That said, as you go through the process, if modifying any of the forms will better address your specific needs then by all means do so. They should be used in whatever way, shape and form serves you for the best results.

Only You can answer the questions posed in this book … make it important enough to do so … and rise to the challenge, and the grand opportunity, of creating good, better and best results for your life. YOU hold the key!

FOR YOUR NOTES, IDEAS, PLANS, INSPIRATIONS ...

Planning the Life You Desire, Living the Life You Deserve

Creating & Achieving Goals That Matter Most

For Best Results ...

Undertake this process in a way that supports you ... a way that will help you get the very best results for yourself. For most people this means being in a setting that is "distraction-free" (cell phones off, quiet, no interruptions). Sitting in a chair or elsewhere that supports your body well is good (though not so comfortable as to make you drowsy!). Having on comfortable clothes can make a difference as well. So can choosing to be in a room, outside area or other spot that just makes you feel good.

NOTE: Studies have shown that playing classical music in the background while studying or reading results in greater retention of information. Yet another option for getting best results as you engage in this invaluable process. *Make it a great adventure!*

Chapter 10 ~ My Purpose In Life

You may be in a hurry to get to the setting of your goals and resolutions. If so, sprint ahead ... how you use this "Tool Kit" is up to you.

However, I'd be remiss to not invite you to also address this key question, as the "umbrella" over your goals and all else: **What is my Purpose in Life?**

Many people have never even considered the question before. Yet it's a pivotal one for how we lead our lives and the meaning that they have. Having a clear and written statement of purpose ... creating it and "experiencing" it regularly ... can indeed be a super powerful thing.

By experiencing it I mean choosing words and phrases that are meaningful to you, that you have strong feelings for, that you're passionate about ... and then feeling them at your core, believing in that purpose fully as you say it aloud (or within) to yourself.

For instance: "My Purpose in Life is to be, do and give my very best, to bring greater goodness to the world and to support those who I have the privilege to touch throughout my life."

So what are you here for? What's your purpose? Say it any way you like, whatever way has meaning and value for you.

My Purpose in Life Is:

_____

_____

_____

_____

_____

"Have you realized that today is the tomorrow you talked about yesterday? It is your responsibility to change your life for the better."

Jaachynma N.E. Agu, The Prince and the Pauper

For Chapters 11 -14 you'll have the choice of completing the forms section by section as they appear in the book or using the blank pages to the left of each section to fill in details ... like the compelling Why for each goal, the strategies and action steps. In the alternative, you can use blank sheets of paper or electronic versions of the forms for this process. Responses for the first 6 forms (pages 37 - 47) can also be consolidated onto a single page if preferred (page 49). Best to **read through the Chapters before getting started** in developing your "answers" so you can gain an overall perspective of the process plus decide which approach will work best for you.

NOTE: After your handwritten "masterpiece" is complete (i.e., all the forms in this book) consider typing it up into a "clean" version that you can keep with you for frequent review. Regular reviews will embed your "destinations" and "roadmaps" in your conscious and (even more important) your subconscious mind, dramatically increasing the positive results you will create.

If you prefer to use our electronic templates for the clean version, see www.CPICorporate.com/workbook-forms/.

"There is only one corner of the universe you can be certain of improving, and that's your own self."
— Aldous Huxley

Chapter 11 ~ My Goals & Priorities

What Do I Want?

The process of creating goals and resolutions first involves identifying the categories or "departments" of life that are relevant and that matter to you. Following are typical **life categories**, in no set order, along with space to add others appropriate to your life if any are missing.

1. Marriage/Relationship
2. Career/Job
3. Family
4. Health & Fitness
5. Personal Growth
6. Spiritual Life
7. Finances
8. Friends
9. Lifestyle
10. Other: _____
11. Other: _____
12. Other: _____
13. Other: _____

Goals & Priorities: What's Most Important to Me?
My Current Focus

Of these same categories, which are the most important in your life <u>at this time</u>? Note to the right of each on a scale of 1 – 5 (with 5 as the most important) the number that best represents that category (not where you may want it to be but) <u>as it actually is right now</u>, based on your life as you're living it, your current focus.

1. Marriage/Relationship
2. Career/Job
3. Family
4. Health & Fitness
5. Personal Growth
6. Spiritual Life
7. Finances
8. Friends
9. Lifestyle
10. Other: _____
11. Other: _____
12. Other: _____
13. Other: _____

Goals & Priorities: What's Most Important to Me?
My Future

Of these same categories, which are the most important for your future? Which, if given the right and best attention, can lead to the kind of future you want? Note to the right of each on a scale of 1 – 5 (with 5 as the most important) the number that best represents that category as you want it to be for your life.

1. Marriage/Relationship

2. Career/Job

3. Family

4. Health & Fitness

5. Personal Growth

6. Spiritual Life

7. Finances

8. Friends

9. Lifestyle

10. Other: _____

11. Other: _____

12. Other: _____

13. Other: _____

My Life Categories

Marriage/Relationship

Career/Job

Family

Health & Fitness

Personal Growth

Spiritual Life

Finances

Friends

Lifestyle

Other: _____

Other: _____

Other: _____

Other: _____

My Ideal Life

IMAGINE: What would it be like to live your ideal life? What would such a life look like? How would it feel? How would you be experiencing it? What results would be showing up? Picture it! Describe your ideal life for the categories at left that matter the most to you.

Goals & Priorities: What's Most Important to Me?
My Goals

Of these categories, which are most important to you <u>for purposes of setting goals and resolutions</u> at this time? Circle or highlight the numbers for the ones that you want to focus on for now. Your "Ideal Life" from the prior page should help. Not choosing an area doesn't mean you don't care about it. It may mean that things are going well in that area to the point that no further action is needed right now. **Choose the focus for your attention and action.** These may be the same as or different from the earlier "My Future" list.

1. Marriage/Relationship

2. Career/Job

3. Family

4. Health & Fitness

5. Personal Growth

6. Spiritual Life

7. Finances

8. Friends

9. Lifestyle

10. Other: _____

11. Other: _____

12. Other: _____

13. Other: _____

Goals & Priorities: What's Most Important to Me?

Priorities

Congratulations. You've chosen the areas you'll be creating goals and resolutions for ... and through them, seeking new results for your life. One more step is needed. Either below OR on the prior page: To the right of the categories that you chose to focus on, assign a number (again, 1 – 5) to indicate your priority for each. Some people will have only a few or maybe just one or two categories to work with; while others will have more, a variety. Consider which are most important for your life at this time (everything being relative). You can pursue as many as you want (whatever makes sense for you) ... and deciding which will receive the greatest focus is important to moving forward.

1. Marriage/Relationship
2. Career/Job
3. Family
4. Health & Fitness
5. Personal Growth
6. Spiritual Life
7. Finances
8. Friends
9. Lifestyle
10. Other: _____
11. Other: _____
12. Other: _____
13. Other: _____

NOTE: See table at right if it's easier for you to provide answers to the prior pages on a single page. See forms for the distinctions between the 5 column names. Some may seem the same but each is actually different.

Prefer to List It All On One Page?

If so, the following table can be used for the answers of pages 37 - 47.

Life Category	Want	Now	Future	Goals	Priorities
1. Marriage/Relationship					
2. Career/Job					
3. Family					
4. Health & Fitness					
5. Personal Growth					
6. Spiritual Life					
7. Finances					
8. Friends					
9. Lifestyle					
10.					
11.					
12.					
13.					

"Go as far as you can see. When you get there, you'll be able to see farther."   Zig Ziglar

Goals & Priorities: What Are My Goals?

For each of the areas you chose to focus on for your goals, you'll find worksheets below for the setting of those goals – as well as defining your outcomes and objectives. But first some important background info to help guide the overall process:

Clear & Written

One of the most important things to know is this: The act of writing down our outcomes, goals and objectives helps us (and forces us) to clearly define them. Having to confine each to a sentence or two brings greater definition as well. Strive for clarity. Vague or "fluffy" statements take us nowhere ... and more specific statements that aren't clear don't get us to where we want to be either.

Having written (hand written or typed) goals also enables us to look at them on a regular basis. Doing so reinforces them within our conscious and subconscious minds in a way that has huge bearing on our achieving them.

Outcomes & Objectives

These two things accompany your goals. For purposes here, outcomes are what you *really* want from the goals, on a "big picture" feeling or experiential basis. Objectives stem from the goals and spell out the shorter term results and direction to make the goals reality.

For our purposes, goals are expressions of desire and intention with a longer term view. They may or may not be quantifiable or measureable. Objectives are more specific and usually measurable. Outcomes provide "the juice" as they tie to our emotions and how our achievements will make us feel. So do the answers to "The Why", coming up shortly.

Examples

"I want to make a difference in the world". That's a great sentiment and desire. But it's not a clear goal. It's more of a broad purpose in life kind of statement. Goals (and objectives) need to be more concrete, more expressive of what it is you're seeking to accomplish. For instance (and see the Appendix Part III for a range of others):

Goal: "To undertake a new career where I can serve and support elderly people through my knowledge and skills in health care".

Objectives:

- "To obtain my nursing degree by April of next year"

- "To be hired as an RN by the Jackson Arms Nursing Home by next summer" (or, "by a nursing home or assisted living facility in my community")

Outcome: "To fulfill my purpose in life as a compassionate and loving person, dedicated to supporting others in need, and to feel happy and gratified by the experience"

These are examples. There is flexibility in how you structure yours. Make them meet your needs. The form is less important than the function.

Other Do's & Don'ts

Don't get hung up on the terms. As discussed in the Appendix, different professionals define and use the above terms in different ways. Focus on getting a valuable plan for your progress, no matter the form.

Think of what you first write down as a draft. Get your thoughts down first. Then refine or revamp it to make it the way you really want.

Concentrate on results ... what do you want things to be like, look like, feel like in your life ... what do you want to have happen? Ask yourself questions like these to bring out the best statements, both for your outcomes and goals.

Make your statements positive wherever possible. If you put what you _don't_ want "front and center" that will become your focus. Focus your words and thoughts on what you _do_ want.

Also choose goals that are within your control, or at least reasonably so. If your ability to achieve them is largely in the control of others (or "the universe") you may or may not be able to reach them ... and you may become frustrated and throw in the towel when obstacles from outside sources get in your way.

Include tangible results where they fit – and especially do so when setting your corresponding objectives: how many or much, what milestone achieved, by what date or time-frame, what standard, etc.

Use terms that resonate with you ... words and phrases that you relate to ... ways of saying things that help you feel the power and energy of the goal (or goal-related statement).

Be specific but concise. More words may be needed for clarity but don't make your statements lengthy or cumbersome. Think about how they will sound to you as you read them and speak them aloud (as part of reinforcing them).

Resources

More examples of goals, objectives and outcomes are in the Appendix (beginning on page 135). They can help you get the ball rolling. BUT remember, your goals should be your own. If simply copied from another source they won't likely have the same meaning and power for you. Focus on the content, the words and the distinctions that matter to you.

First Things First

Read and follow the instructions below. They're presented as they are for a purpose, for the best end results for you. As part thereof, be sure to list the categories first, read on (the instructions) and then return to the forms for your goal setting.

Completing this process is not a race. Make it a priority ... and take the time you need for each part so the results will be most meaningful for your life.

WHAT ARE MY GOALS, OBJECTIVES & OUTCOMES?

Now's the time to get down to it ...

In this part of the process you'll be taking time to craft your goals ... and, as part thereof, to think even more carefully about what you want for your life. What you want will be spelled out as desired outcomes, goals and objectives. As you invest the time and effort here you can create all kinds of possibilities <u>and</u> realities ... by your own design you truly can have so much more.

As a reminder give yourself the gift of a quiet place to think this through and make your notes. Take your time to say it and lay it out the way you want it. This will be the guide for the next phase of your life!

Use the worksheets and format provided below for each of the areas that you said are your priorities for goal setting (your lists from pages 37 - 47 in this Chapter). Answer the worksheet questions on a separate paper if helpful, maybe even a photocopy of the pages (or the backs of the pages of the book are available for this). Then fill out the form in this workbook once you have the statements the way you want them.

If you need support (including specific examples of how to do each), see Part III of the Appendix (beginning on page 135). *You can do this kind of process for your company or organization as well if that applies.*

Also know that setting your resolutions is being made easy through these steps, as you'll be drawing them from the "work" you're about to do on your goals.

Inspirational Insights

Rewrite your major goals every day, in the present tense, exactly as if they already existed. Committing your goals to paper increases the likelihood of your achieving them by one thousand percent!
Brian Tracy

"You can't hit a target you cannot see, and you cannot see a target you do not have."
Zig Ziglar

"Decide what you want, decide what you are willing to exchange *for it. Establish your priorities and go to work."*
H. L. Hungt

"The indispensable first step to getting the things you want out of life is this: decide what you want."
Ben Stein

"You'll never achieve your dreams if they don't become goals."
Anonymous

"It is in your moments of decision that your destiny is shaped."
Anthony Robbins

Ready, Set, Go!

For the forms on pages 59 - 67:

<u>Using the worksheets on these pages, first list the categories</u> that you chose for setting your goals and resolutions (the priority categories only). Place them at the tops of the pages for as many categories as you chose.

Five forms are provided. But there is <u>no set number of categories</u> to do this for. You may have more or less than five. The number depends totally on what you want and what you're able and ready to commit to. That's true for the number of goals too.

Use additional paper if needed for more than five categories (or, when the time comes, for additional goals). You also can amend any of the categories you initially chose, in order to best fit with this planning process in line with your life direction.

After you've written in the category names as noted above, <u>go to the instructions that follow the last worksheet (see page 69)</u>. Wait on completing the rest of the form information until going there first.

When the time comes (through Chapters 13 and 14) you may also prefer to write in your Strategies and Action Steps on the blank pages to the left of each form so that the information is all together ... a further reminder to read the Chapters first before completing the forms.

The categories that we choose for our lives are our focus. They get our greatest attention. The results that we produce stem from them. Select categories that have greatest meaning for where you are ... and where you intend to be.

Category #1: _____

My Desired Outcome Is:

My Goal Is:

My Objectives Are:

Category #2: _____

My Desired Outcome Is:

My Goal Is:

My Objectives Are:

Category #3: _____

My Desired Outcome Is:

My Goal Is:

My Objectives Are:

Category #4: _____

My Desired Outcome Is:

My Goal Is:

My Objectives Are:

Category #5: _____

My Desired Outcome Is:

My Goal Is:

My Objectives Are:

NOTE: Now that you've written your categories on the forms ... see the "Next Steps" on the following page.

Once you've completed the Next Step actions for each of the above forms, head on to 73.

Next Steps

A few general points and then the details for continuing with the above worksheet forms:

General

Once your category names are filled in use the blank pages to take your first shot at defining the details for each category ... by writing out (or noting down the concepts for) <u>your outcomes and then your goals and objectives</u>. Once you're happy with your drafts fill in the worksheet forms.

Complete this process one by one for each of your chosen categories before going on to the next category.

Remember, the outcomes are what you want to experience by way of reaching your goals.

Also remember to identify the driving force for your goals – The Why -- as you go. *If you need help or inspiration on that flip ahead to page 69 then come back here and continue the process.*

My Outcomes

Start with <u>one of the above categories</u>, in no particular order (e.g., whether the most important one to you or the easiest one), to get the process going. Ask yourself the questions:

- What do I want to feel in this category of my life?
- What do I want to experience by taking action in this area?
- What will action in this area of my life mean to me?
- Why is it important for my future?

Whether within the worksheet or on separate paper, note down the answers - whatever comes up for you. Ask yourself repeatedly until you have no new answers. Don't critique the answers as you go. Simply write it all down.

The answers may surprise you ... and they will help you construct powerful statements of outcomes. They will lead you as well to your goals ... and, later on, to your resolutions.

Take your notes and use them to write an outcome statement(s) for your first category. See the earlier example and those in the Appendix if you need help. Follow the instructions below for likewise creating your goals and objectives for the first life category.

My Goals

In similar fashion, for the category you started with above, ask yourself:

- What do I want for this category of my life?
- What do I want to do, have or be?
- What do I want to create, affect or have happen?
- Why is it important for my future?

Same as above: no judgment; note down all the answers; ask until your answers are completed. Then use your notes to write your goal(s).

Use your notes to write <u>one or more goals</u> for your first category. See the earlier example and those in the Appendix if you need help. Note that the forms use singular terms (Outcome, Goal) but each category can include however many are relevant to you.

My Objectives

Again, for the category you started with and the new goal(s) you have created, ask yourself questions like:

- What can I do to achieve this goal?
- What will this goal "look like" once achieved?
- What tangible result will come from achieving this goal?
- What has to show up in my life for this goal to happen?
- What specific action or result will help fulfill the goal?

Once again: no judgment; note down all the answers; ask until your answers are completed.

Use your notes to write one or more objectives for each goal in your first category.

TIP: Glance over the examples in the Appendix (pages 135 - 139) to help you get started – for this part as well as strategies and actions steps.

RECAP: **Proceed with your outcomes, goals and objectives, completing all three for one category at a time.**

Yes, this takes time to do … but the process works wonders … and it's well worth your time since it's about *designing your life*!

Return to page 59 to get started.

Good Luck and Go for It!!

FOR YOUR NOTES, IDEAS, PLANS, INSPIRATIONS ...

Planning the Life You Desire, Living the Life You Deserve

Creating & Achieving Goals That Matter Most

- ❖ How can you celebrate your progress thus far? What's at least one way you can acknowledge yourself?

- ❖ What several steps will help prepare you for getting the most from the next phase of this process?

Your Written Guide

If you've completed your first or final cut for all of the forms, Congratulations! You've taken a huge step forward in designing your future!

If you've done so but you're not happy about, or not quite there, with what you've written ... not to worry. You may need to take more time -- to perhaps "sleep on it" or otherwise allow the opportunity to reflect further and then compose or refine your final written "work".

If you've not done the forms at all, what are you waiting for?

Strongly recommended: once you have completed the Tool Kit process (or whatever parts you have chosen to do) ...

- create a separate document of your final goals and resolutions, with the final narrative (or key parts) consolidated onto a page
- look at it each day and
- read it aloud, or inside, to yourself.

Read it with commitment, vigor, passion ... letting yourself know with certainty that you WILL create the results you have defined.

You can also benefit by compiling a separate document with your outcomes, goals, objectives, resolutions, strategies and action steps ... and reviewing it regularly as well.

Together these documents – the results of your great work – can be used as a **Strategic Plan for your future**.

Inspirational Insights

"The reason most people never reach their goals is that they don't define them, or ever seriously consider them as believable or achievable. Winners can tell you where they are going, what they plan to do along the way, and who will be sharing the adventure with them."
Denis Waitley

"Goals that are not written down are just wishes."
Anonymous

"Nothing can add more power to your life than concentrating all your energies on a limited set of targets."
Nido Qubein

"We all have two choices. We can make a living or we can design a life."
Jim Rohn

"An average person with average talent, ambition and education, can outstrip the most brilliant genius in our society, if that person has clear, focused goals."
Brian Tracy

Goals & Priorities: Why Do I Want What I Want?

Part I of this book talks about "The What, Why & How" ... and how being very clear about Why we want something is crucial to achieving it ... and that identification of the Why (the compelling reason, as put by Stephen Covey) always comes before the How.

Through your actions in the above sections (the worksheet forms), hopefully you've made great headway in figuring out the Why for your goals.

This section, then, can be used as a supplement to that effort, a cross-check of sorts ... and you can also use it to solidify your resolutions (in the next chapter).

In addition to the questions already asked, here are some others worth considering ... ask the ones that are relevant for each of your goals ... and, of course, be sure to note down the answers:

- Why do I want this goal to be achieved?
- What will achieving this goal mean to me?
- What will it mean to others who I care about?
- How will my life change for the better?
- How will I contribute more and better as a result?
- How will doing this achieve my purpose in life?
- What will my life be like if I don't achieve it?
- How much more happiness and fulfillment can I have if I act on this goal right now?
- How much pain will I experience, in one form or another, if I do not?

If there are other questions that help you get at the Why with more clarity and depth, write them down, ask them and note down the answers.

Questions can be framed to bring out the positive aspects of acting, whereby you're drawn toward something you want ... or the negative, whereby you're motivated to act in order to avoid a consequence you don't want.

The answers provide leverage for you to get the results you want.

Structuring your questions well makes an important difference. For example, a smoker may ask: Why should I stop smoking? Or they may ask a different kind of question, like: What will my daughter's life be like growing up if she loses me to cancer? Which of these questions is likely to give them the most compelling answers ... moving them to positive action?

Having compelling information at hand can make a difference in getting you to take action as well. For instance, not just that smoking is unhealthy but (as noted in a great book by Mark Victor Hansen, "The Power of Focus"): "Consider this: If you smoked ten cigarettes a day for 20 years that's seventy three thousand cigarettes. Do you think seventy three thousand cigarettes could have an impact on your lungs?"

The Why also doesn't have to be geared to the most logical answer. For instance, years ago I attended a multi-day event where the diet was vegetarian and the hosts promoted a shift to such foods upon the registrants' return home. They presented a mix of "logical" reasons and statistics – better for our health, better for the environment, etc., all of which I supported but none of which would have resulted in a behavioral change on my part. But when they showed graphic pictures of cruelty to animals in the food production process, that was it. I changed in an instant and I knew I would never eat another piece of meat again. That was over 20 years ago and I haven't. Those pictures (and the feelings they evoked) were all it took and I had my compelling Why.

The form that follows can be used to make sure that the Why's upon which you based each of your goals and desired outcomes are rock solid -- and that they're the most important Why's.

If in asking yourself more questions you discover that some of your goals lack enough foundation and umph, don't feel badly ... get excited! Because it means the answers and the process have served you well.

Be thankful for the Why and use it to get you focused on the outcomes and goals that truly are most important and meaningful for your life.

When you've finished detailing the Why's celebrate having discovered and defined the DRIVE for achieving what you most want for your life.

Why: The Foundation for Your Outcomes

Using the questions in the section you just read, or others if a better fit for you, ask yourself the Why's for each of your draft outcomes. Use additional paper as needed ... and revise your stated outcomes where new discoveries lead you in a better direction. Start with a few words summary for each outcome, then find and state the Why's (below or on the prior Outcomes pages, 59 - 67).

Outcome # 1:

Outcome # 2:

Outcome # 3:

Outcome # 4:

Outcome # 5:

Why: The Foundation for Your Goals

Using the questions in the earlier section, or others if a better fit for you, ask yourself the Why's for each of your draft goals. Use additional paper as needed ... and revise your stated goals where new discoveries lead you in a better direction. Start with a few words summary for each goal, then find and state the Why's (below or on the prior Goals pages, 59 - 67).

Goal # 1:

Goal # 2:

Goal # 3:

Goal # 4

Goal # 5:

Goal 6:

The next page is here should you have additional goals to list ...

Goal # 7:

Goal # 8:

Goal # 9:

Goal # 10:

Goals & Priorities: What Are My "Final" Goals & Priorities?

Now that you've come this far, it's time to **pause, review and reflect**.

Take a look at what you've written.

Do the answers to the Why questions change anything? Especially the question connecting back to your purpose in life?

Do you feel a connection with your outcomes and goals?

Have you covered all the categories?

Do you feel good about the priorities?

Are you happy with – and maybe even excited about! – what you've done?

Do you have any revisions or additions to make it even better?

If so, make them now!

When you're finished, **sign and date the bottom of the pages** that you've created ... as part of your commitment to focus on and meet the goals and objectives you have chosen.

Inspirational Insights

"Goals that are not written down are just wishes."
Anonymous

"When a man does not know what harbor he is making for, no wind is the right wind."
Lucius Annus Seneca

"In the long run men hit only what they aim at."
Henry David Thoreau

"Too low they build who build beneath the stars."
Edward Young

"The person with a fixed goal, a clear picture of his desire, or an ideal always before him, causes it, through repetition, to be buried deeply in his subconscious mind and is thus enabled, thanks to its generative and sustaining power, to realize his goal in a minimum of time and with a minimum of physical effort. Just pursue the thought unceasingly. Step by step you will achieve realization, for all your faculties and powers become directed to that end."
Claude M. Bristol

Google dictionary defines Resolve as to "decide firmly on a course of action" and a **"firm determination to do something"**. Set your sites and resolve with vigor!

NOTE: Some may choose to integrate the goals (with action steps) and resolutions into a single exercise, others will have separate entries. See what fits best for the ideas and desires that come up for you.

Chapter 12 ~ Creating My Resolutions

Resolutions reflect a combination of desired end results and actions that we make a commitment to so that they will happen in our lives.

As reported in a 2012 University study (see Appendix): "**People who explicitly make resolutions are 10 times more likely to attain their goals** than people who don't explicitly make resolutions."

As discussed in Part I, when it comes to New Year's Resolutions most people want to:

- Stop something
- Start something
- Become something or
- Get something

The examples are many, as shown there and in the Appendix below. The Appendix also includes highlights from studies and articles on the top New Year's Resolutions for the year, including statistics on how many people set and keep their resolutions.

The menu of resolution possibilities is vast. Some of the questions that can help in developing them are here:

- What do I want?
- What do I most want?
- What end results are needed to achieve my goals?
- What actions will benefit me most if taken over the next year?
- What actions am I prepared to really commit to?
- How do the resolutions I'm considering relate to my goals, outcomes and purpose in life?

If you've taken the steps in the prior chapters you have just the right foundation for creating your resolutions.

No matter when you make them -- whether at the onset of a New Year or later -- **resolutions represent the potential and the power for positive change** ... for transforming your life for the better.

Look back over your completed worksheets – or if you skipped over the earlier parts of the process, go back through and lay the groundwork for effective resolutions.

<u>Use the next two pages to create yours</u>. As an empowering option, you can set deadlines within the year or other terms for making your resolutions more specific and measurable. You also can use an additional page (as provided) to show the related categories, as you chose for your goals, and make the connections to your goals and purpose. Spelling out those connections in writing will provide even greater motivation for seeing your resolutions through.

<u>Remember</u>: Most people don't keep their resolutions because they don't take reinforcing steps like this!

When you are finished, **sign and date the bottom of the resolutions page** ... as part of your commitment to focus on and keep the resolutions you have chosen.

FOR YOUR NOTES, IDEAS, PLANS, INSPIRATIONS ...

Planning the Life You Desire, Living the Life You Deserve

Creating & Achieving Goals That Matter Most

"The Future Belongs to Those Who Believe in the Beauty of Their Dreams"

Eleanor Roosevelt

"Believe You Can and You're Halfway There."

Theodore Roosevelt

My Chosen Resolutions

I, _____, **commit to the following Resolutions** for the year 20__ (or for the period of: _____).

    1. I resolve to:

    2. I resolve to:

    3. I resolve to:

    4. I resolve to:

Note: The number of Resolutions is up to you. Continue on the next page if you have more. If you only have one or two, that's fine too. They are here to serve you based on your needs and priorities at the time. They can, of course, be added to over time.

"I will be generous with my love today. I will sprinkle compliments and uplifting words everywhere I go. I will do this knowing that my words are like seeds and when they fall on fertile soil, a reflection of those seeds will grow into something greater."

Steve Maraboli, *Life, the Truth, and Being Free*

5. I resolve to:

6. I resolve to:

7. I resolve to:

8. I resolve to:

9. I resolve to:

10. I resolve to:

A dog's New Year's Resolution: I will not chase that stick unless I actually see it leave his hand!   Anonymous

Integrating My Resolutions, Goals & Purpose

Think about how the various "pieces of the puzzle" that you've been working on tie together ... and how your resolutions can help you achieve other elements of your new "Strategic Plan".

My resolutions further my goals, objectives, outcomes and life purpose by:

FOR YOUR NOTES, IDEAS, PLANS, INSPIRATIONS ...

Planning the Life You Desire, Living the Life You Deserve

Creating & Achieving Goals That Matter Most

Some of the Many Timely Covey Quotes

Inspirational quotes from Stephen Covey. Google for many more!

- I am not a product of my circumstances. I am a product of my decisions.

- The main thing is to keep the main thing the main thing.

- Live out of your imagination, not your history.

- The key is not to prioritize what's on your schedule, but to schedule your priorities.

- Most of us spend too much time on what is urgent and not enough time on what is important.

- You have to decide what your highest priorities are and have the courage — pleasantly, smilingly, non-apologetically, to say "no" to other things. And the way you do that is by having a bigger "yes" burning inside. The enemy of the "best" is often the "good."

- **Live, love, laugh, leave a legacy.**

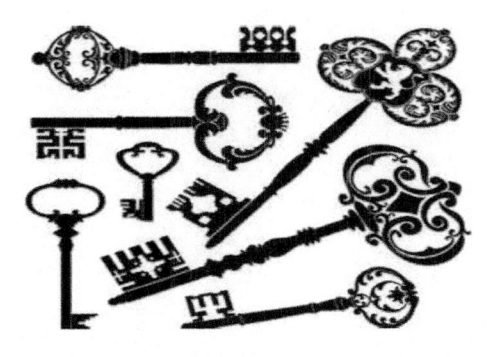

"There are two great days in a person's life - the day we are born and the day we discover why."

William Barclay

Chapter 13 ~ Strategies for Achieving My Goals & Resolutions

Setting goals and resolutions is a huge step forward. But as great as it is there's another crucial ingredient for your success: effective strategies. You can know what you want but if you have no strategies for getting there – or the wrong strategies – chances are you won't make it. Several key questions to help you along the way are:

- What approaches will take me in the direction of my goals?
- What strategies can I employ to achieve my goals?
- What strategies am I prepared to undertake to reach my goals?

Chapter 7 of this book lays out eight overarching strategies for success. The Appendix includes others.

One of the eight that has enormous value is **asking yourself empowering questions** that will lead to your best actions and results. Tony Robbins (whose seminars I had the joy of being a Trainer for, for 10 years) is a master at using this strategy.

Too often people ask themselves questions that have a counterproductive effect, like "Why can't I lose this weight?" The question presumes your failure and thereby contributes to it. Alternative questions to support yourself in your quest could include: "What can I do today to achieve my ideal weight?" or "How great am I going to look and feel when I free my body of 15 more pounds?" or (when you're standing in front of temptation) "What can I do in this moment to support my health and vitality?".

Note that these questions also **focus on what you want rather than what you don't want**, another strategy that can be of great support. Though sometimes the unwanted behavior comes to mind more quickly and easily (like "stop smoking"), setting your sites on a positive vista ahead can draw you toward it more readily. Like, in the case of smoking: "How much more vitality will I have as I clear my lungs and take in only the fresh air?" or "How many years can I add to my life by making better choices on what I put in my body?".

Think of the questions that make sense for you and, again, see Chapter 7 and the Appendix for other strategies for success.

As yet another broad strategy, you may be familiar with the use of Affirmations, positive statements to yourself repeated with regularity that focus on what you want ... as though you already had achieved it. These – and their "cousin", Incantations (or as Mark Victor Hansen calls them, inCANtations) -- focus our minds on what we want in a way that truly helps realize our goals and dreams.

Through a sustained focus our conscious and subconscious minds become partners in creating the belief within us that we can get to where we want to be and that we are in the process of doing so. Through a concerted focus, and new beliefs by design, we begin to real-lize (make real) what we seek.

A few examples of statements using this tool follow:

- For someone who needs to be a better listener and to show more interest in others: "I am a great listener ... I listen with genuine interest ... I focus on listening first ... and I enjoy asking questions to learn about and connect with others."

- For someone financially challenged or who has difficulty accepting abundance: "I deserve, am creating and will soon enjoy financial freedom."

- For someone with a habit that's bad for their health, like smoking, drinking or over-eating: "I show love and respect for myself and for my body as the host that makes all that I do possible."

This simple strategy has worked time and again for me ... and it illustrates that one's path to success doesn't have to be complicated.

We simply need to choose strategies that move us forward and get us results ... and when a strategy doesn't work, to adapt our approach to another that will.

That means that we also need to keep an eye out for what is and isn't working by monitoring and evaluating our strategies and action steps.

In addition to the broad strategies come those that are specific to individual goals.

Formulate and define your strategies on the next page ... or on the blank pages next to the prior forms for Outcomes, Goals and Objectives, pages, 59 - 67. If here, first recap each goal in a few words.

Specific examples of Outcomes, Goals, Objectives, Strategies and Action Steps appear in the Appendix (starting on page 135).

"By recording your dreams and goals on paper, you set in motion the process of becoming the person you most want to be. Put your future in good hands — your own." –Mark Victor Hansen

The Strategies for Achieving My Goals Are:

Goal # 1:

Goal # 2:

Goal # 3:

Goal # 4

Goal # 5:

Good ideas and good intentions are great to have ... but Action is required for them to be turned into positive results.

Chapter 14 ~ Action Steps: The Steps to Carry Out My Charge

One of the biggest reasons that people fail to achieve their goals and resolutions is that they fail to identify the steps involved in implementation.

Action Steps are the specific "next steps" involved in making what we want happen.

Identifying these steps is the means of moving from simply knowing your target to actually reaching it. The steps become the pathway for our success, the method of materializing it.

Unfortunately, most people neglect this part of the picture. We may think of one or two things to do to pursue what we want. But we tend not to task ourselves to be systematic and complete about it. Hence, we get results that only partially take us there, if at all.

Stopping smoking for a week, dieting for a bit only to return to one's old ways, deciding to change jobs or careers but searching for a time then giving up ... these are a few examples of what happens when we don't plan for and take effective action.

Breaking down the specific steps that can take us to where we want to be is crucial.

Without defining the steps our course is random and aimless. With the steps it is clear, focused and purposeful. We know what to do each day, week and/or month to move forward.

Forward movement also creates momentum that inspires more forward movement.

By laying out the steps, and taking them, we create the opportunity for a new life.

Map out your Action Steps here ... or on the blank pages next to the prior forms for Outcomes, Goals and Objectives, pages 59 67. If below, first recap each goal in a few words.

Specific examples of Goals, Objectives, Strategies and corresponding Action Steps appear in the Appendix (pages 135 - 139). Best to consult them first to get the best value for this important part.

The Action Steps for Achieving My Goals Are:

Goal # 1:

Goal # 2:

Goal # 3:

Goal # 4

Goal # 5:

FOR YOUR NOTES, IDEAS, PLANS, INSPIRATIONS ...

Planning the Life You Desire, Living the Life You Deserve

Creating & Achieving Goals That Matter Most

Having a plan is not enough. You must implement the plan – take action on it – for it to have real meaning.

Chapter 15 ~ Implementation: Achieving Ultimate Success

Congratulations again for making it this far. The opportunity for success, in whatever that term means for your life, awaits you through this next step ... the step of pulling it all together and making it happen.

Am I Resolved?

Being resolved means being committed and determined. So some questions to ask of yourself here are:

- How committed am I?
- How can I be even more committed?
- What am I willing to do to show my commitment?

By now you should have already mapped out where you want to be and how you plan to get there. So test yourself with these questions. Be sure that you really want what you've said you want ... and that you're determined to make it happen.

Hopefully you're certain. If not, head back to the Why (the motivation for your actions) and "up the ante" ... get clear again on why you must and will take the necessary actions to achieve what you said you wanted ... or determine if you really want something different and why, then chart out the plan for it.

You can become even more committed by coming up with even more reasons why you're determined to reach your goals ... not just why you "should" but why you are really ready to say and know that you will and must reach them. Imagine them coming true ... and allow yourself to feel the excitement about making them your own.

Say It, See It, Feel It, Be It

From this place, **say aloud and with vigor what you're willing – and what you're going -- to do**, in general and specifically. Perhaps things like:

- "I care about myself and I'm willing and ready to make this year's Resolutions <u>happen</u>" (come true, become reality, materialize, etc. – whatever words ring true for you) ... OR ...
- I am willing, ready and <u>absolutely committed</u> to making my resolutions become my reality."

These are the general statements to get you going. Some more specific examples follow:

- "I am creating a better life by <u>taking time for myself each day</u> to support my health and happiness ... by exercising, improving my diet and having an empowered focus."
- "I deserve to have a successful new business and <u>nothing will stop me</u> in making it happen."
- "I will attract the relationship of my dreams by knowing what I want and being the best me ever."
- "I am taking charge of my financial future, creating financial abundance as a way of supporting my family, causes I believe in and the life I so richly deserve."

Making statements like this aloud and with conviction each day will help get and keep your resolve solid as can be ... keeping you on the path to your best success.

A variation of this approach that can bring even better results is to word the statements as though what they are saying <u>has already happened</u>. Close your eyes and <u>See</u> the destinations you seek as being real ... vividly imagining them, and feeling them, as though they have happened. Doing so will draw you to them, and to their realization, like a magnet. Your subconscious mind will believe them to be true and will work to bring the conscious mind to follow suit.

Work Your Plan

Of foremost importance here (assuming that you now have a plan) are:

1. Write it down
2. Read it daily
3. Read it with vigor
4. Follow through

As noted elsewhere, be certain that you **write down** your Purpose, Goals, Objectives and Resolutions ... as well as your Strategies, Action Steps and Outcomes. Together these constitute your personal Strategic Plan. If you went right to the Resolutions part of the Tool Kit, then write them up and the key elements of your plan for them. Written statements of support – affirmations, incantations, visualizations, empowered commitments – will also serve you well for "working your plan".

Read what you wrote, at least once daily. The more times you input it to your brain, your thoughts -- and to your subconscious (which soaks it up for important use in supporting you) – the better able you'll be to create new results for your life.

Read it like you mean it. Saying it with energy, with a sense of enthusiasm, with belief, with optimism ... these steps have enormous value in making what we want come to reality.

You don't have to believe the above is true in starting out ... just believe that you're worth it ... trust ... and have faith that good things will come from your action.

Form new habits. We're all "creatures of habit" who become "stuck in our ways" as part of our "comfort zones". But many of the areas where we want new results necessarily involve shaking up what we're accustomed to and changing old habits. Experts say it takes practicing a new behavior or habit 21 – 30 days, after which it becomes the "new normal", what we're comfortable with. So know that there is "light at the end of the tunnel" … by resolving to "find it".

By taking the above steps you will be ready to **follow through** … so be true to yourself and "just do it"!

A Reminder

This is <u>very important</u> so bears repeating:

It's strongly recommended that, once you have completed the Tool Kit process (or whatever parts you have chosen to do), you create a separate sheet (keeping it to one page if possible) that shows your final Goals and Resolutions … look at it each day … and read it aloud, or inside, to yourself.

Read it with commitment, vigor, passion … letting yourself know with certainty that you WILL create the results you have defined.

Put the page some place where you really will look at it every day – whether taped to a mirror, in a folder on your night-stand, in a plastic display stand (from an office supply store), etc. Looking at it more than once per day is even better.

Allow what you see and read aloud to become ingrained in you … to become a part of you … to create the future that you want … and Will have.

And return to this process, and what you create from it, year after year. In its best form, life is an ongoing process of growth and change for the better ... and the process set forth in this book is intended to facilitate the most positive of growth.

"We first make our habits, then our habits make us."
John Dryden

No matter what we do or what we want, **"results" are always produced** ... they're either good results, bad results or somewhere in between. Monitoring one's results enables celebrating progress made and adapting plans & actions where improvements are needed.

Chapter 16 ~ Monitoring My Progress

As with most plans it's important to keep an eye on how you're doing and adapt your course as needed along the way to get better and best results.

For each of your goals and resolutions determine how you will track progress and evaluate how you're doing. The tracking is vital to your noticing what's working and not working, and how well your strategies and action steps are performing.

If your strategies and actions are not paying off, or not quickly enough or reasonably so, it may be time to switch to another course of action that will do more and better.

Being attentive, flexible and timely in this regard will produce valuable returns.

Some questions to ask yourself follow on the next page … and, again, you can create your own as tailored to your specific needs.

Ask yourself on a regular basis … monthly, quarterly and annually is great … a look-see daily or weekly is even better.

Be diligent in your reviews, honest in your answers, fair in your approach.

Be Diligent. It's easy to get off course by not taking these steps. But you've come too far to not invest in this final step!

Be Honest. Hold yourself accountable for the results you defined and the course you embarked on. You made a commitment. Have you been sticking to it?

Be Fair. If you've not come as far as you intended, don't beat up on yourself. Seek instead to understand what happened ... and identify solutions for moving forward.

Set up a system for tracking your performance and the results of your actions. Whatever system works for you – the form below, an Excel spreadsheet, a handwritten journal, a typed report perhaps with verbal presentation to a loved one (as a testimonial, perhaps giving them permission to give feedback aimed at keeping you on track) or another tool or process that supports you and your goals.

Noting down the timing of your reviews and your findings provides a baseline to help you see and gauge your progress ... and the information to take other action if needed.

Monitoring My Progress, Evaluating My Results

How Am I Doing?

Over the next several pages are a series of questions for you to ponder and answer as a means of sizing up where you are and, based on that, what to do next.

<u>Overall</u>, **how do I rate my progress** to-date on a scale of 1 – 10 (with 10 as the best)?

What's the basis for the number I chose?

FOR YOUR NOTES, IDEAS, PLANS, INSPIRATIONS ...

Planning the Life You Desire, Living the Life You Deserve

Creating & Achieving Goals That Matter Most

In the following pages, consider: What positive results have I produced or progress have I made?

Monitoring My Progress, Evaluating My Results

Am I moving closer to or further away from my desired outcomes? How so?

Outcome # 1:

Outcome # 2:

Outcome # 3:

Outcome #4:

Outcome #5:

Monitoring My Progress, Evaluating My Results

How am I doing on each of my goals? Am I moving closer to or further away from their achievement? How so?

Goal # 1:

Goal # 2:

Goal # 3:

Goal #4:

Goal # 5:

How am I doing on each of my resolutions?

Resolution # 1:

Resolution # 2:

Resolution # 3:

Resolution #4:

Resolution # 5:

What's Working?

What else can you add about how you're doing – in particular, things that are working well? For instance: What have I done that I'm pleased with? What steps have I taken, what strategies have I used, what priorities have I chosen that are paying off with positive results?

What Needs Improvement?

What Can I Do Next? What will bring about improvements, get even better results, make me (and others) feel better in the process? What other questions do I need to ask to move to a higher level?

You may also want to use pages 104 – 106 (or prior blank pages) to fill in the details next to your evaluations of Outcomes, Goals and Resolutions.

"The art and science of asking questions is the source of all knowledge." Thomas Berger

Chapter 17 ~ Bonus Resources

Bonus Questions

Questions are a powerful tool for manifesting what we want in our lives. They help bring clarity and focus as well as new answers that we wouldn't otherwise have thought of. They can create many new possibilities for achieving our aspirations.

Some additional questions in support of your progress and future follow:

- What does "success" mean to you?
- What will it take to have real success in your life?
- What has to happen for you to feel a greater sense of success in your life?
- What actions on your part could most fulfill your purpose in life … your life's potential?
- What does your ideal day look like?
- What does your ideal life look like?
- What kind of person do you need to be in order to create your ideal life?
- How will you know when you have it?
- What are you willing to do to have and keep it?
- When is a great time to read and speak your goals and resolutions?

Add some further questions of your own on the page at left.

Free E-Tips

The subconscious mind has enormous power, to support or defeat our goals and dreams ... depending on how we use it. It's at work whether we consciously tap its power or not.

I learned about its functions and great power many years ago from books and audio tapes of Zig Ziglar. His teachings had a life-long impact on me and played a big role in the launch of my company all those years back.

The free downloadable e-tips at the link below provide great insights into how we can put our own subconscious to work in our support. They're based on my separate e-book shown below.

To collect your copies, go to: http://www.creative-pursuits.com/Subconscious_Power.html.

Power of the Subconscious Mind
Thank You Zig Ziglar

by Marcia Elder

Other Timely Resources

Thanks for the chance to serve you through the content of this book and the process that you've engaged in. My company and I welcome further supporting you in the future. **Call on us if you (or someone you know) needs related support in the areas below** or through other services noted on our Websites, such as these (and others):

- Personal Coaching (live online, by phone or in person)
- Strategic Plan Development (business or personal)
- Personal or Professional Development Training
- Business Evaluation & Coaching

For a free published article that I wrote a few years back, "What Does It Take to Stay in Business Over 25 Years? Top 10 Insights from a Small Biz CEO" go to: http://creative-pursuits.com/News.html

Come for a visit to these sites and feel free to email or give us a call:

www.CPIConsulting.co   TheVirtualSolutionsCenter.com

www.CPICorporate.com   www.MarciaElder.com

850.997.2837   support@cpicorporate.com

Remember to also check out the APPENDIX below PLUS other timely information at the close of the book ... and be sure to use this process to do something GREAT for yourself, now and for the rest of your life.

Thanks for the opportunity to serve you in your process of growth and creating the best results for your future.

Marcia Elder

Inspirational Insights

"People with goals succeed because they know where they're going."
Earl Nightingale

"When defeat comes, accept it as a signal that your plans are not sound, rebuild those plans, and set sail once more toward your coveted goal." — **Napoleon Hill**

"I don't care how much power, brilliance or energy you have, if you don't harness it and focus it on a specific target, and hold it there you're never going to accomplish as much as your ability warrants." — **Zig Ziglar**

"Obstacles can't stop you. Problems can't stop you. Most of all, other people can't stop you. Only you can stop you." — **Jeffrey Gitomer**

"You can conquer almost any fear if you will make up your mind to do so. For remember, fear doesn't exist anywhere except in the mind." — **Dale Carnegie**

"Whatever you can do, or dream you can, begin it. Boldness has genius, magic, and power in it." – **Johann Wolfgang Von Goethe**

"Do not wait; the time will never be 'just right.' Start where you stand, and work with whatever tools you may have at your command, and better tools will be found as you go along." — **Napoleon Hill**

Appendix

Included here is supplemental information to assist you further, including: some general background on strategic planning; interesting findings from others on the resolutions people set ... and what happens to them; and a sampling of more Outcomes, Goals, Objectives, Strategies and Action Steps as a further guide for your actions.

I. General Background

Planning Terms & Processes

It can be easy sometimes to get bogged down in the terminology of a process ... and that's something we want to avoid in this book. Some people get confused with personal and business planning lingo – whether the distinctions between goals, objectives, outcomes, purpose and mission ... or terms like milestones, benchmarks, tactics and others.

The proper uses for certain terms are sometimes even debated. Some tend to get used inter-changeably, like outcomes and goals instead of goals and objectives.

It can be said that your goals are a way to achieve desired outcomes – and your objectives, strategies and actions are the more specific means for fulfilling both. As noted earlier, goals are generally the broader, longer-term statements and objectives provide the details for the short term and are measurable.

Some also would say to limit an outcome or goal to one concept, whereas some of the examples in earlier Chapters have more than one. In Chapter 11 the first goal, for instance, includes: new career, helping the elderly and providing health care. However, integrating these three elements is what provides the clarity and focus that our hypothetical "Mary" wants and needs ... and a very meaningful set of objectives for her naturally stems from this goal statement.

Regardless of the terms and form, **what's important here is clearly identifying what you want in a way that will help you achieve it.**

II. Resolutions: In the News

Excerpts from several related resources on the subject are here ...

Wikipedia says about New Year's Resolutions:

"A New Year's resolution is a commitment that a person makes to one or more personal goals, projects, or the reforming of a habit. A key element to a New Year's resolution that sets it apart from other resolutions is that it is made in anticipation of the New Year and new beginnings. People committing themselves to a New Year's resolution generally plan to do so for the whole following year. This lifestyle change is generally interpreted as advantageous."

A **December 2012 University of Scranton study** reported the following Resolution priorities for 2012:

Rank	Top 10 New Years resolutions for 2012
1	Lose Weight
2	Getting Organized
3	Spend Less, Save More
4	Enjoy Life to the Fullest
5	Staying Fit and Healthy
6	Learn Something Exciting
7	Quit Smoking
8	Help Others in Their Dreams
9	Fall in Love
10	Spend More Time with Family

In addition they found:

Type of Resolutions (Percent above 100% because of multiple resolutions)	Data
Self Improvement or education related resolutions	47%
Weight related resolutions	38%
Money related resolutions	34%
Relationship related resolutions	31%

They go on to say that 45 percent of Americans usually make New Year's Resolutions ... and they note that only 8% of people are successful in achieving their resolutions. (*To that we say, all the more reason to have an **effective system for creating and achieving resolutions**.*) They did report, however, that "resolutions maintained through six months" were at 46%. Details on their findings are here:

http://www.statisticbrain.com/new-years-resolution-statistics/

A recent article on **About.com** (Pittsburgh) points to the **"Top 10 New Year's Resolutions"** as follows:

1. Spend More Time with Family & Friends
2. Fit In Fitness (get fit!)
3. Tame the Bulge (lose weight)
4. Quit Smoking
5. Enjoy Life More
6. Quit Drinking
7. Get Out of Debt
8. Learn Something New
9. Help Others
10. Get Organized

Details at: http://pittsburgh.about.com/od/holidays/tp/resolutions.htm

Health.com featured this article on December 31, 2012: "Top 10 Healthiest New Year's Resolutions", including:

1. Lose Weight
2. Stay in Touch (with people)
3. Quit Smoking
4. Save Money
5. Cut Your Stress
6. Volunteer
7. Go Back to School
8. Cut Back on Alcohol
9. Get More Sleep
10. Travel

For details:
http://www.health.com/health/gallery/thumbnails/0,,20452233,00.html

This Forbes article (published December 31, 2012) presents "Seven Strategies for Highly Effective New Year's Resolutions":

http://www.forbes.com/sites/margiewarrell/2012/12/31/seven-strategies-for-highly-effective-new-years-resolutions/.

III. Sample Plans

Specific examples of Outcomes, Goals, Objectives, Strategies and Action Steps follow.

Reminder: These are here to assist you in developing your own, not using these. For goals and objectives in particular to have *umph* ... for you to personally connect to them and have the drive to go after them ... they need to be tailored to your needs, priorities and circumstances. And again, the form of what's here isn't set in stone. Learn from what we've provided in the Tool Kit ... and set up your statements in whatever form best serves you.

Category: Career/Job

Desired Outcome: To create and feel great about having a more balanced life with much more time that I "can call my own".

Goal: To change jobs so that I can spend more time with family and more time for myself doing activities that I enjoy and that support my well-being.

Objective 1: Find a new job within the next 9 months where I can work close to home (with limited or no travel), work up to 45 hours a week, enjoy and be fulfilled by what I'm doing and make at least 90 % of my current salary. OR

Objective 2: Start a family-owned business doing work that my spouse and I enjoy, that the kids can take part in and that will be a good investment.

Two alternatives are shown for this category and ones that are not mutually exclusive, such as if the business was small and part-time doing something that the family enjoyed. It could later lead to something larger and could involve other family members. The sample Strategies and Action steps that follow are focused on Objective 1.

Strategies:

- Identify the kind of work that I enjoy, that would be fulfilling to me, that I'm good at and that meets my needs for more time with family and more time for me.
- Identify employers in my area that employ people in those kinds of jobs.
- Identify specific ways by which I can effectively promote myself to prospective employers.
- Determine my expectations and requirements for accepting an available job.

Action Steps:

1. Prepare a comprehensive list of the kinds of work I could enjoy and find fulfilling. *For instance, types of employers, roles, assignments and activities, even if they're different than what the person has done before.*
2. Write down how doing this kind of work would make me feel.
3. Prepare a comprehensive list of what I have to offer an employer. Identify my experience, skills, values and other important assets.
4. Visit a job search site(s) online and look at the categories of career fields and job types shown. Peruse specific openings to get a broader feel for the range of career employment options. Make a new list of the types of work and jobs that appeal to me.
5. From the above list, identify those where I do, could or might qualify for a job.
6. Identify employers in my geographic area that have jobs of those types and list the ones of interest (or possible interest) to me.
7. Look up the Websites for companies and other organizations of interest and check the career/job sections of those sites weekly.
8. Use search engines to check each day (*or whatever frequency fits*) for jobs of possible interest.
9. Update my resume – and check online for articles with good tips on how to do so effectively.

10. Sign up on one or more social media Websites geared toward career and job networking and do regularly posts (at least two weekly) to keep my name out front.
11. Develop "talking points" to use in presenting myself to prospects and network contacts in an effective way.
12. Apply, apply, apply.

The above are all examples. The list can go on or be abbreviated. It is to be tailored to your specific interests, needs and commitments. Other examples follow for yet another category, Health & Fitness.

Category: Health & Fitness

Desired Outcome: To be healthy, feel vibrant and look good

Goal: To restore my health, fitness & endurance to where it was 5 years ago

Objective 1: Lose 15 pounds in the next 6 months.

Objective 2: Increase my running speed on the track by 1 minute per lap in the next 60 days.

Objective 3: Increase my aerobic activities by doing a 60 minute workout twice per week.

Objective 4: Resume lifting weights at least 3 times per week for 10 minutes at a time.

Objective 5: Increase my daily intake of fluids by 16 ounces.

Objective 6: Learn about and make healthier meal and snack choices.

Objective 7: Reduce my TV time and go to bed an hour earlier to get better sleep and wake up feeling energized and ready for an active day.

Strategies:

- Become a vegetarian.
- Create and consume a balanced daily diet.
- Make and drink fresh vegetable and fruit drinks.
- Join a fitness club that provides instruction and motivational support.
- Lift weights at home while I'm doing other things (for best use of time and for motivation, distraction).
- Invite friends to exercise together and commit to encouraging each other to achieve our goals.
- Ask my family to support me in getting the rest I need so I can be my best for all of us.

Action Steps:

Body/Weight/Appearance

1. Weigh myself on day 1 and every 7 days after. Keep note of my weight. Keep a notebook next to the scale.
2. Buy a fabric tape measurer. Measure my waist, hips, thighs and upper arms on day 1 and every 14 days after. Add notes to my notebook of changes.
3. Look at myself in a full length mirror and every 14 days after (wearing bathing suit or underwear). Add notes to my notebook of changes I observe.

Dietary

1. Buy 2 vegetarian cookbooks and identify recipes that sound appealing to me.
2. Locate and eat at 2 vegetarian/vegan restaurants and identify dishes on the menu that appeal to me or sound interesting to try. Note them down and inquire about the ingredients.
3. Identify other local restaurants that serve vegetarian meals.
4. Identify foods that I will eliminate or reduce from my diet and identify others that I will replace them with.
5. Become a member at the local health food co-op/farmer's market and shop there once per week.

6. Make a supply of vegetable and fruit snacks each week and keep them in the refrigerator ready to go. Turn to them when I think of unhealthy snacks.
7. Buy a "Magic Bullet" and use it to make fresh fruit and/or vegetable drinks. Drink at least one such drink per day.
8. Resume taking my vitamin/mineral supplements, and keep them on the kitchen counter as a reminder.
9. Invite friends over once per month to prepare healthy meals and exchange recipes.

<u>Exercise</u>:

1. Research local fitness clubs online, by calling and by asking friends. Visit my top choices and select the one that will work best for me.
2. Rearrange my daily schedule so I can take part in exercise and fitness activities without stress; and devote my full attention to them while I am there.
3. Hire a personal fitness coach for a month (4 sessions) and have them help me with specific strategies and forming new fitness habits.
4. Ask Patty and Rick to run with me once per week. Tell them my speed goal and run to at least that level.
5. Choose TV shows that I like a lot and schedule my weight lifting sessions when they are on. Keep the weights in the family room ready to go. Add stretches to my routine as well. Invite my husband and kids to join in ... and, whether they do or not, enjoy my own progress while I'm enjoying my shows and making great use of my time.

From these examples and other information in the Tool Kit, you should be all set to develop your own Outcomes, Goals, Objectives, Strategies and Action Steps ... and, in the process, to design your life for a new and exciting future.

The ability to do so rests within you. Awaken it to full strength and put it to work now for the very best results in your New Year and each year ahead!

Inspirational Insights

"If you want to be happy, set a goal that commands your thoughts, liberates your energy and inspires your hopes."
Andrew Carnegie

"It doesn't matter where you are coming from. All that matters is where you are going."
Brian Tracy

"Do not let what you cannot do interfere with what you can do."
John Wooden

"You miss 100 percent of the shots you don't take."

Wayne Gretsky

About the Author

Marcia on top left pole! (see below for the why!)

Marcia Elder is a long-time professional consultant who has headed her own company for over 25 years, a multi-disciplinary consulting firm called CPI Consulting (originally founded as Creative Pursuits, Inc.). The firm was created with a focus on personal and professional development. It later grew to provide expert services in strategic communications, the virtual environment (online events and more) and other professional services. Marcia's mission, and that of her company, is one of facilitating and supporting positive change for a better world. Find out more at the Websites below.

Marcia was a Trainer for Anthony Robbins' seminars for 10 years and the photo above is from her very first event, a "massive" personal growth experience! Participants climb the very high pole, figure out a strategy for getting on top (with nothing to hold onto) then jump for a trapeze!

Within each of us lies the opportunity to be empowered and to design our lives in ways that reveal and fulfill our purpose.

Marcia Elder

About the Publisher

Want to publish your own book or e-book and have it be available worldwide like this book? Contact "**CPI Corporate**" for excellence in service. They can handle your publishing needs quickly, efficiently and in a way that will make you all the more proud of your published book ... plus help you with marketing it as well.

CPI also creates Websites, social media campaigns, online interviews, Web-based videos, online events and other ways of getting visibility and customers for your books and other products or services.

Find out more at: www.CPICorporate.com

Your Review Is Requested

If you followed the process in this book then we're confident you found it valuable. Please take a moment to leave a review here, even if brief: www.CPICorporate.com/review-the-book/

Check Out Other Books by Marcia Elder

Visit Amazon.com for these additional books by this author:

"The Resolutions Tool Kit: Creating & Keeping New Year's Resolutions" - $7.99, Kindle
The Resolutions Tool Kit is a powerful tool for making positive changes in your life. It's designed to be your guide and support in doing so, through the steps you'll be taking in setting and achieving Resolutions.

Resolutions can be set at the start of a New Year ... or at any time. The important thing is to create them and make them happen. The Tool Kit is totally user-friendly. And it's based on the assumption that the user, You, is ready to take action in support of your future.

"New Year's Resolutions: Creating & Achieving Your Goals for the New Year & Beyond" - $1.49, Kindle
Setting and seeking to achieve New Year's Resolutions can be one of the most important actions of a person's life. This powerful e-book provides the "what, why and how" of doing so.

Resolutions are statements of resolve ... pinpointing actions that a person "resolves" or commits to take. Their purpose is as a tool for achieving new end results in our lives, to make things better in one way or another.
Though typically developed at the start of the year, they can have great value no matter when they're set ... so long as they're accompanied by effective strategies for making them real, making them happen.
Learn about how to create meaningful goals, resolutions and strategies for your life.

See www.MarciaElder.com for more ... plus:

Inspirational Insights

"We must walk consciously only part way toward our goal and then leap in the dark to our success."
Henry David Thoreau

"Reduce your plan to writing... The moment you complete this, you will have definitely given concrete form to the intangible desire."
Napoleon Hill

"Go as far as you can see, and when you get there you will see farther."
Orison Swett Marden

People become really quite remarkable when they start thinking that they can do things. When they believe in themselves they have the first secret of success.
Norman Vincent Peale

Motivation is a fire from within. If someone else tries to light that fire under you, chances are it will burn very briefly.
Stephen R. Covey

Coming Soon through Amazon.com ... a book that may not seem related – because a pack of 9 giant breed Great Pyrenees dogs is at the center of it – but it stems from a life-changing personal growth experience of the author that actually does relate to the kinds of questions and purposes of "Creating the Life You Desire".

The name of this book has not yet been released but you'll be able to find it soon by searching under the author's name.

This book will be preceded by a mini version that introduces readers to the doggies. That version will be released before Christmas of 2015 ... and will make for warm and inspiring holiday reading and visuals.

Planning the Life You Desire, Living the Life You Deserve

Creating & Achieving Goals That Matter Most

Other Timely Resources

www.CPIConsulting.co

www.TheVirtualSolutionsCenter.com

www.CPICorporate.com

Upward & Onward for Your Best Success